FISHING: TIPS & TECHNIQUES™

BASS FISHING

SIMONE PAYMENT

rosen publishing's
rosen central®

New York

Published in 2012 by The Rosen Publishing Group, Inc.
29 East 21st Street, New York, NY 10010

Library of Congress Cataloging-in-Publication Data

Payment, Simone.
Bass fishing / Simone Payment.—1st ed.
        p. cm.—(Fishing: tips & techniques)
Includes bibliographical references and index.
ISBN 978-1-4488-4598-9 (library binding)
ISBN 978-1-4488-4604-7 (pbk.)
ISBN 978-1-4488-4735-8 (6-pack)
1. Bass fishing—Juvenile literature. I. Title.
SH681.P38 2011
799.17'73—dc22

                                                                    2010048415

Manufactured in Malaysia

CPSIA Compliance Information: Batch #S11YA: For further information, contact Rosen Publishing, New York, New York, at 1-800-237-9932.

CONTENTS

*B*ass fishing is a fun, easy, popular, and relaxing hobby. It is also a great opportunity to spend time outdoors. As a hobby, bass fishing has many advantages. It can be done alone or with others. Because bass are found in lakes, ponds, streams, and rivers, it is possible to fish in many different bodies of water all around the United States and Canada. It's possible to fish for bass from the shore of a small stream or in a specialized bass fishing boat on a large lake. There's no need to buy a lot of equipment to fish, although tools and gadgets that make finding and catching fish easier are available. Another plus is that fishing can be done most of the year. In most parts of the United States and Canada, anglers can fish in the spring, summer, and fall. In southern parts of the United States, bass fishing is a year-round activity.

Striped bass live in coastal ocean waters. There are several different types of bass, and they can be found in many types of environments. Largemouth and smallmouth bass can be found in lakes, ponds, rivers, and streams in most parts of the United States and Canada. Other types of bass—such as

spotted bass, white bass, and white perch—are also found throughout the United States and Canada.

Bass fishing can be a lot of fun, but with a bass fishing hobby comes responsibility. The natural environment is endangered in many places, and fish populations are in decline. Pollution and over-fishing are serious problems. Both have affected many types of fish—including freshwater and saltwater bass populations—and the environment as a whole. It's extremely important to take care of and improve nature in its current state. This will ensure good fishing in the years to come.

CHAPTER 1

BASS FISHING BASICS

Before starting to fish, it's helpful to know more about fish and their habits. Learning about where they live can provide information on what kind of fish might be found in nearby bodies of water. Knowing what they eat can help determine what bait to use and when to fish.

What Is a Fish?

Fish are cold-blooded, vertebrate animals. This means that they have a backbone (vertebra) and their body temperature adjusts to match the temperature of their surroundings. Fish breathe through gills, which are flaps of skin located on either side of the head. Fish must move through the water in order for the gills to work. As water flows through the gills, they absorb oxygen from the water.

Fish—like this largemouth bass—can't breathe outside of the water because their gills can only absorb oxygen from water.

A fish's fins and muscles power it through water. Scales protect the body, and a coating of mucus over the scales offers defense against infection. The mucus coating also helps fish move through water quickly.

To help them find food, fish have well-developed senses. They have excellent senses of smell and hearing. They are able to taste with their mouth and tongue, but also with the exterior of their body. Fish can also sense food via vibrations in the water. Fish are able to see well. Most can see in many directions because their eyes are near the top of their heads.

Types of Bass

There are several types of bass. They are so different that some bass live in freshwater and others live in salt water. The two major types of freshwater bass are largemouth and smallmouth. Other bass that live in freshwater are spotted bass, white bass, and white perch. Striped bass begin their lives in freshwater, but as adults they spend most of their time in salt water.

Largemouth

Largemouth bass are the biggest type of bass. They are a very popular North American fish, partly because they put up a good fight, which can make them a challenge to catch. Light green or brown on top, largemouth bass have a white stomach with dark spots shaped like diamonds on their sides. Largemouth bass are usually between 5 and 10 pounds (2.3 and 4.5 kilograms) when full grown, but can weigh as much as 20 pounds (9 kg).

Smallmouth

Smallmouth bass are the second largest type of bass. Like the largemouth, they put up a good fight while being caught. They are usually a bit thinner and smaller than largemouth, and they have a smaller mouth. Smallmouth bass are brown, gold, or olive green. They are lighter on their sides and have a white belly. Unlike the largemouth, smallmouth bass have red eyes. Smallmouth bass range in size, but can be from 2 pounds to 6 pounds (1 to 3 kg) when full grown.

Other Freshwater Bass

There are several other types of freshwater bass. The spotted bass is often confused with the largemouth bass because they look similar. However, spotted bass are smaller. Other ways to tell them apart are that spotted bass have teeth on their tongue and a large spot near their gills.

White bass also put up a good fight and are a good fish for eating. They are usually silver with a dark gray or green back. They have yellow eyes and several dark stripes that run along their sides.

Although it might seem from the name that they are part of the perch family of fish, white perch are actually bass. Like white bass, they are very good for eating. White perch look similar to white bass but have a thin body. They can be olive, grayish green, brown, or even black on their backs, with light green or white on their belly. Although most white perch live in freshwater, they can also live in salt water or brackish water, which is a mixture of salt and freshwater.

Striped Bass

Striped bass are large and have a long body. They are bluish black or dark green on top with a silver or white belly. Black stripes run along their sides.

Unlike most types of bass, striped bass live most of their lives in salt water. As adults, they live in coastal ocean waters. But when female

Most striped bass spend the summer in cooler northern waters, then swim farther south for the fall, winter, and spring.

striped bass are ready to lay eggs, they swim up freshwater rivers connected to the ocean. After they lay their eggs, they swim back out to the ocean. Any eggs that aren't eaten by other fish or predators hatch in the river. The hatchlings spend their early lives in the river. Eventually, the young striped bass swim out to the ocean.

Some striped bass live their whole lives in freshwater. Some of these freshwater striped bass were moved by people to inland freshwater lakes and rivers, and survived to breed and start new populations. Other freshwater striped bass populations began when the Santee and Cooper rivers in South Carolina were dammed in the 1940s. Striped bass in those rivers at the time were trapped but adapted to the conditions.

Where to Fish for Bass

When deciding where to fish, the first thing to do is check local fishing regulations. Fishing is prohibited in some areas and bodies of water. There can also be restrictions based on the season, so a fishing area may be open at sometimes, but not others.

A great way to locate a good fishing spot is to ask a local angler. He or she will be able to point out not only a good body of water,

Bait and tackle store employees can be an excellent source of fishing information—even if they keep the very best fishing spots to themselves!

but possibly even the best spot on that body of water. To find a local angler, talk to friends or family, or ask at a bait shop or store that sells fishing gear.

If a fishing spot turns out to be a good one, make a note of its location. Also note what time the fish were biting, the weather conditions, and the bait used. This information can help when planning a future fishing trip.

Largemouth

Largemouth bass live in many types of bodies of water throughout the mainland United States and a few southern areas of Canada. They can be found in small creeks or ponds, but more often they live in lakes, larger ponds, and rivers. They like fairly warm water, of about 70 degrees Fahrenheit (21 degrees Celsius) or higher.

Largemouth bass occasionally look for food near the surface of the water. However, largemouth bass usually stay well below the surface of the water. They especially like darker water, so they are often found in shady areas, such as below branches or trees that have fallen into the water. They can also be found near low-hanging branches, or underneath lily pads. However, largemouth bass will usually only be found in these areas if the water is a few feet deep or more.

Smallmouth

Smallmouth bass prefer clearer water than largemouth bass. They also like water with a rocky bottom, so they are most often found in streams or clear lakes. They are also happier in cooler water than largemouth bass—about 65°F (18°C). Smallmouth bass can be found throughout most of the United States. They are also widely found in Canada.

Smallmouth bass are fun to fish because of their habitat, which is calmer streams and clear lakes.

Other Freshwater Bass

Spotted bass live most often in streams. White bass live in large lakes or rivers. White perch can be found either in salt water near the shore and coastal rivers or freshwater lakes and ponds. White perch like to be close to the bottom of any body of water.

Striped Bass

When they are in the ocean, striped bass are usually near the shore. They like to look for food around bridges, docks, and piers, and around rocks. Striped bass spend most of their time looking for food around these structures and near the bottom, but they will come to the ocean surface if they are chasing food. When striped bass are in freshwater to lay eggs, they are usually in the open water in the middle of a river.

The largest populations of striped bass are along the East Coast of the United States. However, there are smaller populations along the Gulf Coast and in the Pacific Ocean off the coast of the northern United States and southern edge of Canada.

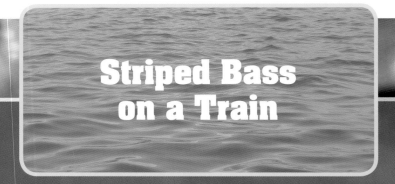

Striped Bass on a Train

The striped bass that live along the West Coast of the United States got to that area in an unusual way. They were originally brought by train from New Jersey to San Francisco, California, in 1879. While only 132 fish survived the long train trip, 300 more were brought a few years later. Eventually, there was a thriving population of striped bass along the northern California, Oregon, and British Columbia, Canada, coast. There are not as many now because the coastal rivers where females used to lay their eggs have been dammed to irrigate local crops.

What to Use as Bait

Two types of bait can be used when fishing for bass: live bait and lures. Small fish, insects, or other things that a fish would eat in its natural environment are examples of live bait. Live bait can be purchased from a bait or fishing shop or can be caught. Lures are artificial, but are made to look somewhat similar to natural bait. Bait shops and local anglers can offer good advice on what kind of live bait or lures to use.

Live Bait

Live bait includes worms, crickets, grasshoppers, crayfish, and minnows. It can be found at bait shops and sometimes at fishing shops or other local stores. In some areas, bait can even be purchased from vending machines.

Bait can also be in caught easily most areas. Worms can be found in nearly any yard, especially after a rain or at night. To keep worms alive and healthy until it is time to fish, make sure they are cool and damp by adding some soil, moss, or damp newspaper to the container, and leave airholes in the container.

Crickets or grasshoppers can be found in tall grass and caught with a small net. Keep insects cool and dry with some grass or dry newspaper in a container with plenty of airholes. Crayfish can be caught in shallow water near rocks with a net. Minnows can also be caught in shallow water with a small net or minnow trap. Store crayfish or minnows in water until ready to use.

When using live bait, put it on the fishing hook in a way that won't kill the bait. This way, it will still move in the water and attract a fish. At the first hint of a nibble on the line when using live bait, tighten the line to "set the hook" in the fish's mouth. Waiting too long will allow the fish to possibly swallow the bait.

Worms are easy to find or buy. It's also easy to raise them to create a steady supply for fishing. There are many Web sites dedicated to providing information on raising worms.

Lures

Lures can be made of several types of material. Some look like minnows and are made of metal. Some look like worms, frogs, or other animals. There is also a type of artificial bait called flies. These are made of thread and other fiber, and they mimic insects. Lures and flies can be purchased at local bait or fishing stores or online. When using lures and flies, set the hook quickly, at the first bite from the fish. Otherwise, the fish may realize that the lure is artificial and will lose interest.

For Freshwater Bass

Largemouth bass eat a wide variety of food, so many types of bait can be used. They most often eat smaller fish and crayfish. They will also eat frogs, mice, salamanders, snakes, and worms. Live bait like minnows and crayfish will attract largemouth bass, but lures will usually work as well.

Smallmouth bass eat whatever they can find. Their favorites are small fish and crayfish, but they will also eat worms, ants, grasshoppers, ladybugs, leeches, and snakes. Like largemouth bass, smallmouth bass can be caught with live bait or lures.

Spotted bass eat insects, minnows, frogs, worms, and small fish. Crayfish, however, are their favorite food source. White bass eat smaller fish and a variety of insects and crayfish. White perch eat small fish, crabs, and shrimp.

For Striped Bass

Striped bass are not picky eaters. They will eat smaller fish, squid, worms, and crabs. They are happy to eat live bait but will eat dead bait, too. Although eels and clams aren't what they usually eat, chopped eels and clams can be used to attract striped bass.

Many anglers like to fish in the hours just before dark. Fish are usually biting then, and it can also be a great way to enjoy a beautiful sunset.

When to Fish for Bass

The best time to fish varies by location. Asking local anglers when they have had luck can be helpful. Many fishing Web sites can also provide useful information. Some state and local environmental agencies post local fishing information on their Web sites.

In general, the cooler weather of spring and fall is best for freshwater bass, but bass can also be caught in the summer. In some southern locations, bass can be caught in the winter months, too.

Cloudy or overcast days usually make for ideal fishing weather. Another good time is just before it rains. However, it is not usually good to fish after rain, or when it is windy, because the water is stirred up too much. Most bass prefer to feed when the water is clearer. Early to mid-morning is usually the best time of day to fish. The last few hours before sunset can also be a productive time to fish.

CHAPTER 2

BASS FISHING EQUIPMENT

As with any hobby, there are lots of extras that could be purchased, but these are usually unnecessary. Fishing requires very little specialized clothing or safety equipment. There are a few things any angler will need, though. A pole, fishing line, hook, and bait are the basic required items.

Rods, Reels, and Hooks

A fishing pole is a piece of wood with fishing line and hook attached to the end of the pole. A pole can be as simple as a tree branch or piece of bamboo. A pole is easy to make, or it can be purchased. Because there is no reel to control the fishing line, with a pole an angler flicks the line into the water. When a fish bites, simply pull the fish out of the water.

These lures, called plugs, crankbaits, or wobblers, mimic the movement of live bait when pulled through the water on a fishing line.

Rods are man-made, and they have a spot to attach a reel of fishing line. Guides run the length of the rod to keep the line in place. Rods are usually made of fiberglass.

Fishing line is usually made of nylon and is a single strand (called a monofilament). Most fishing line is clear, but it comes in other colors including red, blue, green, and yellow. There are different strengths of fishing line, and each strength can hold up to a certain amount of weight. The number on the package tells how many pounds a particular line can hold.

This spin-casting reel partially encloses the fishing line, which prevents tangles and snags.

There are several types of reels to hold fishing line. Spin-casting reels are the easiest to use. They attach to a fiberglass rod, and the fishing line is enclosed within the reel. Spin-casting reels sit on top of the fishing rod.

Spinning reels take a little more practice to use. The fishing line is not enclosed in a spinning reel, so it can get tangled. The advantage is that it is possible to cast farther out into the water with spinning reels. They attach to fiberglass or graphite rods and sit on the underside of the rod.

Professional bass anglers often use bait-casting reels. The reel winds the line from side to side, not around in a circle. The advantage of using a bait-casting reel is an angler can be more specific about when to release the line. However, the fishing line can easily get tangled, making this type of reel difficult to use. Bait-casting reels are used on fiberglass or graphite rods and attach to the top of the rod.

There are two types of hooks: single and treble. Single hooks, which are used for bait, have just one hook. Treble hooks have three hooks and are most often used with lures.

Hooks are sold with and without barbs, which are sharp points at the tip of the hook. It is best to buy barbless hooks because they cause much less damage to the fish. If barbless hooks are not available, file the barbs off of the hook with a metal file. Or, bend the barb "closed" using pliers.

Other Basic Equipment

In addition to the gear an angler will absolutely need to have, there is other equipment that can make fishing easier. Snap swivels are clips that are attached to the end of the fishing line. These swivels allow anglers to easily put hooks or lures on the line without having to cut the line or tie new knots each time. The snap swivels move around freely so that the fishing line does not become twisted when hooks and lures move through the water.

Sinkers attach to the fishing line above the hook to help the hook sink to the bottom. Bobbers have the opposite effect. They can keep part of the line afloat so that the hook does not sink too deeply. Bobbers can also alert the angler when a fish hits the hook because they move on the surface of the water.

Tackle boxes store the small equipment—hooks, lures, sinkers, snap swivels, bobbers, and so on—an angler needs on fishing expeditions. Tackle boxes can be especially handy when using lures. They keep lures separated and can prevent hooks from getting tangled. Tackle boxes are available in stores, but it's also possible to make one out of a box

The compartments in a fishing tackle box help keep gear organized and safe. Fishing equipment can easily become tangled if not kept separate.

with an egg carton inside it. Small squares of Styrofoam make good storage material for hooks.

A knife for cutting bait or line is useful. Gloves are also usually something an angler will need. Cotton gloves that can be dipped in water are good for handling fish when removing hooks. Thicker gloves can be worn when cleaning fish in preparation for eating.

Some anglers use nets to lift fish out of the water. However, nets can cause a lot of damage to fish. If a net must be used, plastic nets are the best type. These cause much less damage to the fish's protective mucus coating.

Making Fishing Gear

It isn't absolutely necessary to buy equipment in a store. With a little time and creativity, it's possible to make some basic fishing gear from materials found in a backyard or local woods. A tree branch can be turned into a fishing pole. Willow and bamboo are the best pole materials because they are very flexible. Fibers from dead trees or palm leaves can be braided together to create fishing line. The best trees from which to get fibers are willow, oak, or basswood.

Hooks can be made from thorns, sharpened wood, or an opened safety pin. A small piece of bark or wood tied to the fishing line a few feet above the hook makes a good bobber. Grubs or beetles for bait can be gathered from rotting logs, worms can be found underground, and crickets can be caught in tall grass.

The Extras

Sonar and GPS are two types of technology that can be very helpful when fishing. Sonar is also called a depth finder, fish finder, or depth sounder. It shows the underwater environment on a video screen, allowing anglers to "see" the bottom, large objects, and schools of fish.

A GPS, or global positioning system, is a navigational device. GPS systems used for fishing are the same devices that are used in a car.

GPS systems can help locate docks, marinas, and stores where fishing gear and bait can be purchased.

A GPS can help find a specific fishing area if coordinates are already known. Another good use of GPS is "marking" a productive fishing spot. Recording the fishing spot's coordinates will make it easy to find on the next fishing expedition. Some GPS systems are so small and portable that they can be used even on rowboats or canoes.

Bass fishing can easily be done from the shore, a dock, or a riverbank. But many anglers fish from canoes, rowboats, or small engine-powered boats. There are also boats specifically designed for bass fishing. These are most often used by professional bass anglers or other serious anglers. Bass fishing boats are usually very fast, fairly flat on the bottom, and made of fiberglass. The flat bottoms allow the boat to go faster and get close to shore in shallow areas. Bass boats have low, flat deck areas in the front and back to make it easy to fish on all sides of the boat. Flat decks also allows anglers to fish standing up. Bass boats usually have a lot of storage space below the deck and are equipped with sonar and GPS.

Clothing and Safety Equipment

Waders can be worn when an angler will be standing in a stream or a lake to fish. They keep an angler dry and can offer some protection from cold. They can also make it easier to walk on the slippery or muddy bottom.

Taking rain gear or a warm jacket on a fishing expedition is always a good idea, even when rain is not expected. Rain can occasionally arrive unexpectedly, and weather conditions can change quickly on the open water of a large lake or the ocean.

One of the most important pieces of safety equipment any angler should have is a personal flotation device (PFD), or life preserver. Anglers should always wear one in a boat or while wading in a stream or river. Even good swimmers should wear a PFD.

CHAPTER 3

SPORTSMANSHIP AND SAFETY

Respect for fish and for the environment should be top priorities for any angler. Catch-and-release fishing is one very important way of practicing good sportsmanship and environmentalism. Staying safe on the water is another important goal.

Being a responsible angler is one of the most important aspects of fishing. If every angler practices good sportsmanship and conservation practices, fishing can continue to be an enjoyable hobby for many years to come. Poor sportsmanship and irresponsibility can result in damage to the environment, declines in fish populations, and, eventually, fewer opportunities to fish.

Using common sense should be first and foremost, and "think before acting" is a good rule of thumb. Be aware of local rules and be aware of the surroundings. This includes

Preventing problems due to water pollution is easy if everyone does his or her part. If a trash can is not available on-site, bring trash home and dispose of or recycle it.

staying off private property—land, docks, and beaches. Don't get too close to other anglers when fishing from shore. In a boat, don't get too close to docks, the shore, wading anglers, or other boats.

Another aspect of sportsmanship is taking care of the natural environment. At the end of a day of fishing, it is essential to bring all hooks, fishing line, bait containers, and other garbage home to dispose of or recycle it properly. Collecting hooks and fishing line is especially important. Fish, shore birds, and other aquatic creatures like turtles or salamanders can swallow hooks or become tangled in fishing line. This can kill them or prevent them from finding or eating food.

Another way to protect the environment is to only clean fish at home or in specific fish-cleaning stations provided on some docks and marinas. Don't clean fish on a public dock or even along the shore.

Practicing good sportsmanship also means being ethical. Ethics is not the same as legal versus illegal. Instead, ethics concerns what is right versus what is wrong. Just because there is no specific law against something doesn't necessarily mean it is right to do it. For example, most anglers consider it unethical to catch and keep fish that are laying eggs. This is because it interferes with egg laying and eventually lowers the population of the fish. In most states, it is not illegal to catch fish while they are laying eggs. But in some locations, waters where fish are known to lay eggs are closed to fishing during the spring.

Catching too many fish is also considered unethical, even if a particular angler has kept only the limit allowed. If every angler keeps the limit on every fishing trip, it could be harmful to the long-term survival of the fish population.

Another way to practice ethical angling is to not pollute fishing waters or any other area. Even if there is no law in place to prevent a specific type of pollution, it is in everyone's best interest to keep bodies of water and the surrounding environment clean.

Fish this size are too small to keep. Returning young fish to the water benefits the fish population, as well as future anglers.

Catch-and-Release Fishing

Catch-and-release fishing is the practice of returning fish to the water after they are caught. This allows them to live and reproduce, resulting in a strong fish population. Not all fish survive when released, but giving the fish a chance to live is better than not. But giving the fish a chance to live is better than not. Good catch-and-release practices can give a fish a better chance of survival.

Catch-and-Release Rules

There are both official and unofficial rules about keeping a fish versus throwing it back. Some anglers have their own unofficial rules about when to keep or not keep a fish. For instance, some never keep fish. Some keep only a certain number per month or year. Others make their personal rules based on the size or rarity of a fish. Many anglers always return rare or particularly big fish to the water. These larger, older fish are better able to breed and increase the fish population. Some anglers make the decision to catch-and-release a big fish out of respect for the fish and its ability to survive and reach a large, healthy size.

Official catch-and-release policies vary by type of fish or even by the body of water. For example, anglers might be allowed to keep a fish of a certain length from one lake, but not a fish of the same length from a lake just a mile or two away. Environmental officials usually make policies based on the fish population in a particular location.

Chances of Survival After Catch-and-Release

Most fish can survive when they are released back into the water. However, just the stress of being caught or handled can cause fish to die.

There are some factors, or a combination of factors, that can make it more likely that fish will die. Avoiding the following things can increase a fish's chances of survival. First, because fish breathe through their gills, an injury to a fish's gills, even a minor one, is something anglers should try to avoid. Keeping the fish out of the water for as short a time as possible is also essential.

A long fight can cause a substance called lactic acid to build up in a fish. This makes it difficult for the fish to process oxygen. So, bringing the fish to the surface with a minimum of fighting time is a good practice.

The kind of bait used can also affect a fish's chances of survival. Live bait is usually worse for fish because they swallow it more deeply and the hook then causes more internal damage.

Although the angler is not able to control this, where a fish is hooked also makes a difference in its survival. Fish hooked in the mouth, jaw, or cheek generally have the best chances. Fish hooked in the eye or gills usually have a decreased chance of survival.

Successful Catch-and-Release Practices

There are several things an angler can do to increase a fish's chance of survival after being released. Most importantly, if at all possible, keep fish in the water when removing the hook. A good rule of thumb is that fish should not be out of the water longer than twenty seconds at a time. This is probably easiest when fishing from shore, rather than on a boat. But even on a boat it is possible to leave the fish in the water when removing a hook.

Most bass are strong and put up a good fight when being caught. But it is usually easy to handle them because they don't squirm too much. Keep the fish still by gently holding its tail or, preferably, its jaw. (Remember to

This largemouth bass was hooked through its lip, which should make the hook and lure easy to remove. If a fish swallows a hook, removal can be difficult.

avoid touching a fish's gills.) If possible, anglers can work in teams with one angler holding the fish and the other removing the hook.

Most of the time, hooks usually do not go in too deeply in bass, so they are fairly easy to remove, especially if they're barbless hooks. To remove the hook, use a pair of long-nosed or needle-nosed pliers to gently ease the hook out of the fish's mouth. It is sometimes possible to simply put some slack in the fishing line for the hook to come right out. If the hook does not come out right away using pliers or slack in the line, don't tug or pull hard. This can rip the fish's mouth or gills.

Ted Williams on Catch-and-Release Fishing

Ted Williams was a famous Red Sox player and noted World War II pilot. He was also a lifelong angler who fished all over the United States. During his many years of fishing he noticed fewer and fewer fish in the waters he fished regularly. In a 1989 essay in *Popular Mechanics* magazine, he wrote about the need for catch-and-release fishing and other measures to preserve fish populations and the environment. In this quote, he describes catch-and-release fishing: "The first time you set a big one free feels kind of strange, maybe even a little painful. But the next one is easier and after that, they're all easy. You don't have to have a dead fish to prove you caught it. You know you did, and that's all that's important."

If a fish is deeply hooked, some experts recommend cutting the line and leaving the hook inside the fish. This works best if the hook is in the throat and not all the way into the stomach. However, leaving a hook inside a fish will usually greatly reduce the fish's chances of survival. This is especially true for saltwater fish like striped bass because the hook can rust in the salt water.

Although working quickly is important, it's also important to work carefully when removing the hook. It is easy for a hook still attached to a wriggling fish to become caught on a piece of clothing or a hand or finger.

It is not always possible to keep the fish in the water when removing the hook. If this is the case, pick the fish up gently while wearing damp cotton gloves. Or, put a damp towel or cloth over the fish's head or body to handle it. Wearing damp gloves or using a towel does less damage to the mucus coating that protects the fish from infection. Keep a gentle, but firm hold on the fish. Don't let the fish flop around on the ground or the bottom of the boat. This can cause a lot of damage to the fish. It also makes it more likely that the hook can become caught on a person.

Once the hook is removed, the fish can be released. If the fish is already in the water, simply let go of the fish and it will swim away. If the fish is not already in the water, never throw or toss the fish back in the water. Instead, gently place it in the water.

If the fish is not moving much, it may be stressed. If this is the case, hold it gently in the water, keeping it upright. Moving the fish forward will allow water to flow through its gills. This can help revive it. If the fish is in a river, let the fish go with the current, not against it. When the fish begins to move on its own, gently release it.

Water Safety

Because fishing takes place in and around all kinds of bodies of water, good water safety practices are essential. Perhaps the most important

This angler is gently holding a bass in the water to allow it to revive before releasing it. Moving it slowly forward in the water can help revive a fish.

rule of water safety is: always wear a PFD. It is not enough to have a PFD on the boat or nearby. It can be too difficult and sometimes too late to put one on if a boat capsizes. Even good swimmers should always wear a PFD. When buying a PFD, make sure it fits snugly but not too tightly.

Knowing how to swim is a valuable skill for any angler. Many schools or recreation programs offer swimming lessons. If possible, take water safety classes at school or from a local Red Cross or other program. Water safety classes can teach procedures for how to help someone who has fallen overboard or how to flip an overturned canoe.

Anglers should also be familiar with any body of water being fished. This is especially important in rivers. Be aware of the current and how strong it is. Sometimes, the surface of a river or stream looks calm, but underneath the water is moving quickly. Watch out for objects like logs or branches floating downstream.

Also be alert when fishing on the shore of the ocean. Sometimes, particularly near rivers that flow into the ocean, the tide can come in or out quickly. When this happens, water can rise or lower swiftly, leaving anglers in unsafe conditions.

The bottom of most bodies of water is often slippery, so take care when walking. Take small steps, planting feet firmly. Try to put feet between rocks rather than on top of rocks because rocks can be covered with algae or other slippery material.

In a lake, be aware of how deep the water is before wading in along a shore. Use a stick to find the bottom of the lake to measure the depth.

Being careful in and around boats is another aspect of water safety. Don't overload a boat with people or equipment. Make sure there is safety equipment on board. This should include a first-aid kit, lights, a horn, and PFDs for everyone on the boat. When navigating, be alert for other boats, obstacles, dams, rocks, and sandbars. Knowing an area well before taking a boat trip is a good idea. Also watch the weather conditions. Strong winds, high waves, and thunderstorms can be dangerous for any size boat.

Whether in a boat or on shore, watching out for thunderstorms is extremely important, especially during the summer months. Check the forecast before heading out for a day of angling. If thunderstorms are in the forecast, consider changing the day or time of the trip. Thunderstorms can also come up quickly, so even when a thunderstorm is not in the forecast, keep an eye on the skies. Using radios or electronic

Always keep an eye on changing weather conditions when on open water. Get off the water as quickly and safely as possible when a thunderstorm is approaching.

devices like smartphones to get updates on the forecast while angling is a good idea.

If thunder can be heard, don't delay: take shelter. A building or a car is the best place for shelter. If neither is available, try to find the lowest place and stay near the smallest trees. If in a field, stand in an open area, but away from tall trees, telephone poles, or metal fences or posts. Take off anything made of metal.

A warning sign that a lightning strike is imminent is that the hair on a person's arms or head will stand on end. If this happens, kneeling with hands on knees, bent forward is the best position. This gives lightning the least amount of contact with the ground.

Equipment Safety

Some fishing equipment is sharp, so be safe and alert when working with hooks and knives, for example. Even parts of fish, such as fins, gills, and teeth, can be sharp, so take precautions. Only use a knife with clean, dry hands. Or, wear gloves for extra protection. Be alert when using a knife, especially in a boat, which can move suddenly. Also be alert when someone else is using a knife to avoid coming in contact with the knife by accident.

Using barbless hooks is a good idea not only for the sake of the fish, but also for the angler. Barbless hooks are less sharp. Barbless or not, always secure a hook on the line guide of a pole and make sure the line is tight when the pole is not in use. Or, remove the hook from the line.

When handling fish, avoid touching fins, which can be sharp. Gills can also be sharp. Wearing cotton gloves when handling live fish, as mentioned previously, protects the fish. But even dead fish should be handled with gloves to avoid cuts and scrapes.

Legal Requirements

Every angler should be familiar with local laws and regulations. It is the responsibility of the angler to know which fish it is permissible to catch and if there are size or amount limits on those fish. Anglers must also know whether or not a license is required for fishing.

In some states, it is illegal to catch a particular type of fish. If caught, those fish must be released immediately and in good condition. This is usually to protect a rare or endangered type of fish. Limits might also be set to protect fish with a low population in a particular area.

Some states set length limits. For example, a law might require that any fish under 6 inches (15 cm) in length be released.

http://dnr.wi.gov/fish/regulations/2010/documents/FishingRegs10-11_web.pdf#limsmbassmgmtzones

OPEN SEASONS, LENGTH LIMITS, and BAG LIMITS

GENERAL INLAND WATERS

*Remember: Also check the *Special Regulations–Listed by County* section, the Great Lakes, the Winnebago System Waters, the Boundary Waters tables, and the Tributary Streams to Green Bay and Lake Michigan table.

FISH SPECIES–species not listed have no open season.	OPEN SEASON (all dates inclusive)	DAILY LIMIT	MINIMUM LENGTH
LARGEMOUTH BASS and SMALLMOUTH BASS			
Northern Zone (see map on page 9)	May 1–June 18	0 (catch and release only	
	June 19 - March 6	5 in total	14 inches
Other inland waters	May 1 – March 6	5 in total	14 inches
ROCK, YELLOW (STRIPED) and WHITE BASS	open all year	none	none
PANFISH: BLUEGILL, PUMPKINSEED, SUNFISH, CRAPPIE and YELLOW PERCH	open all year	25 in total	none
BULLHEADS and ROUGH FISH (see definition on page 20)	open all year	none	none
CATFISH (CHANNEL, FLATHEAD)	open all year	10 in total	none
CISCO and WHITEFISH	open all year	25 pounds plus one more fish of either species in total	none
MUSKELLUNGE (INCLUDES HYBRIDS)			
Northern Zone: Inland waters north of U.S. Hwy 10 (excluding Wis.-Mich. boundary waters)	May 29 – Nov 30	1	34 inches
Southern Zone: Inland waters south of U.S. Hwy 10	May 1 – Dec. 31	1	34 inches
NORTHERN PIKE			
Northern Zone: Inland waters north of US Hwy 10 (excluding Wis-Mich. boundary waters)	May 1 – March 6	5	none
Southern Zone: Inland waters south of US Hwy 10	May 1 – March 6	2	26 inches
PADDLEFISH (SPOONBILL CATFISH)	Closed all year–no fishing for paddlefish.		

56

Local regulations specify when fish can be caught, how many—if any—can be kept, and how long they must be.

Many states put limits on the number of fish of a certain type caught in one day. Other laws might apply to when fish can be caught. Some fish have seasons when they cannot be caught. This does not apply to most types of bass, except striped bass in some cases.

Fishing licenses help fund conservation and other state efforts to protect fish and enforce rules. Each state has its own fishing license, and anglers must be licensed in the state where they want to fish. Some states issue different permits for saltwater and freshwater angling. Anglers under a certain age may not need a license. There are usually reduced license prices for children and teens if a state does require a license. Licenses are good only for a certain length of time. Some states issue licenses that are valid for one season, or for one full year. Others issue licenses for one calendar year.

Fishing licenses can be purchased from local department of fisheries and wildlife offices. Most states also allow anglers to buy their licenses online.

CHAPTER 4

HANDLING THE CATCH

As discussed in earlier chapters, it is best to practice catch-and-release fishing. It is more humane and better for the health of the fish population. However, in some cases, an angler might choose to keep a fish to eat, as long as it is permitted by local fishing regulations. Be sure to check local sources to make sure it is safe to eat fish caught in a particular body of water.

Storing the Fish

To prepare a fish for eating, the first priority is keeping the fish cool until it can be cleaned and cooked. Put the fish on ice as soon as possible after it is caught. The best way to store the fish is in a cooler with ice and a bit of water. This will keep the fish not only cool but moist as well.

It is best to clean and fillet fish as soon as possible after catching them. If that's not possible, keeping them cold is essential.

Preparing the Fish

Fish should be cleaned as soon as possible. Clean fish at home or in a designated fish-cleaning station at a dock or marina. These stations will have water and facilities to dispose of guts and skin and bones. These fish parts smell and attract flies and other insects, so they must be stored and disposed of quickly. Never clean a fish on a beach or dock or other public area.

When cleaning fish at home, make sure to dispose of the discarded parts quickly. Wrap them well in plastic bags that can be sealed or knotted, and put them in tight, outdoor garbage cans. The smell of dead fish attracts animals, such as raccoons, bears, dogs, or coyotes, so use garbage cans with tight lids.

Cutting a fish for eating is called filleting. Filleting separates the skin and bones of a fish from its flesh. It is not an easy thing to do, but with some practice, it gets easier. However, it is best to have help from an adult or other experienced person for the first few attempts at filleting.

A sharp knife is essential for filleting. Wear a pair of gloves for protection from sharp parts of the fish and from the knife. Also, fish tend to be slippery, so wearing gloves can provide a firmer grip.

A Fish Souvenir

Some people like to keep their fish forever, especially if it is particularly big. A process called taxidermy preserves a fish and mounts it so that it can be hung on a wall. This process was more common in the past, when not as many people practiced catch-and-release fishing. Today, skilled taxidermists can create replicas of fish that look as real as the real thing, but do not require an angler to keep the fish. To create a replica, a taxidermist needs to know the fish's weight and length and coloring. Taking a picture and quick measurements of a fish before releasing it can provide enough information for a taxidermist to create a souvenir of a prized fish.

When filleting, start where the head meets the body. Begin cutting along the back, about 1 inch (2.5 cm) deep to reach the backbone. Pull the meat away from the ribs toward the stomach. Then cut the skin of the stomach down toward the tail, leaving the tail on. Turn the fish over and hold the tail. Slip the knife between the skin and the meat of the fish, and work from tail to head. Repeat this process on the other side of the fish.

Cooking and Eating the Catch

When deciding whether or not to eat a fish, keep in mind that it is best not to eat too many fish from the same area. This is because some

A filleting knife can make cleaning and filleting a fish much easier. Remember that it's best to wear gloves when preparing a fish.

waters contain contaminants that are stored in a fish's body. These contaminants, especially mercury, can be harmful to humans. Check with state or local environmental offices about local bodies of water and safe amounts of fish to eat from them.

Bass are not too fatty, but it is still a good idea to get rid of as much fat as possible because the fatty parts of fish are where contaminants are stored. Good cooking options for burning off fat are grilling or broiling. Special grilling baskets or pans can make grilling a fish easier. Fresh fish tastes so good that it's usually only necessary to cook it with a little olive oil or butter and some salt and pepper.

CHAPTER 5

FISHING AND THE ENVIRONMENT

Fishing is a great way to enjoy the beauty and quiet of nature and all it has to offer. But it is the responsibility of every angler to keep the environment clean and fish responsibly. If we don't protect the natural environment and fish stocks, there may be many fewer fish to enjoy in the future.

Declining fish populations and mercury contamination are two major problems that should concern every angler. They are serious problems, but they do have solutions.

Declining Fish Populations

Fish populations are in decline due to overfishing and pollution. Preventing both is within human control, so it is important for every angler to help prevent these problems and be a part of the solution.

The Great Lakes, and many other bodies of water around the United States, are polluted and in need of cleanup, as illustrated by this fish washed ashore.

One reason fish populations are in decline is due to overfishing. When a species is fished too much, there are not enough fish left to reproduce and keep the population at a steady or increasing level. Overfishing is a particular problem for commercial fishing of popular eating fish, such as tuna, swordfish, and cod. However, even sport fish, such as bass, are in decline. The major way to counteract overfishing is to always practice catch-and-release fishing. Take care of fish so that they can return to the water in healthy condition and continue to reproduce.

What Does a Fish and Wildlife Officer Do?

For people who love the natural environment, becoming a fish and wildlife officer can be an excellent career choice. Fish and wildlife officers usually work for state or national organizations. They issue hunting, fishing, and boating licenses and enforce local and national laws. Fish and wildlife officers often interact with the public. They teach classes on hunting or fishing safety and rules and good conservation practices. Fish and wildlife officers also work with animals and other wildlife. They perform wildlife counts in a particular area to keep track of populations. They also rescue injured animals or capture animals that have entered populated areas.

The other contributing factor to declining population is pollution. Some chemicals that enter the water can kill fish immediately. Other chemicals and pollution reduce the amount of oxygen in the water. Over time, the oxygen level can become so low that fish are not able to survive.

Although the major way large amounts of contaminants enter bodies of water is through pollution from factories or manufacturing plants, individuals can help prevent pollution. Don't dump anything in bodies of water. When fishing, don't leave garbage or other pollutants behind that might find their way into the water. Learn about local companies and potential pollutants that might harm the water. Encourage local officials to make stronger antipollution laws and regulations.

Mercury Contamination

Mercury is a chemical that enters water supplies mainly from mercury particles in the air. The particles are then washed into the water by rain. Once in the water, mercury enters the bodies of fish and aquatic animals. Mercury remains in the organism's body, and if that animal is eaten, it enters the body of the animal that ate the contaminated organism. This means that fish (or animals) that eat smaller organisms have higher mercury concentrations in their body. When humans eat these fish or animals, mercury contaminates our bodies as well.

Because many types of bass eat lots of smaller organisms, they often contain high concentrations of mercury. Largemouth, smallmouth, and striped bass are on the U.S. Environmental Protection Agency's list of fish that should not be eaten by children and pregnant women. Teens and adults should only eat these types of fish occasionally.

Always check with local officials to determine whether it is safe to eat fish. This sign in Florida warns anglers of local mercury contamination.

What Individuals Can Do

There are many things individuals can do to protect the environment and help keep fish populations healthy. First, fish responsibly. Pay attention to—and carefully follow—all regulations about where and when to fish. Consider always practicing catch-and-release fishing. Don't leave garbage behind in a fishing area, and collect the garbage others may have left behind. When boating, be careful not to harm the natural environment. For example, avoid damaging aquatic plants with a boat's motor, and don't spill gas or oil.

Individuals can also educate friends and family about environmental problems that affect fishing. Start a club at school or in the community to promote safe fishing practices. Or, consider a career as a fish and wildlife officer. Fishing can be an enjoyable and relaxing pastime. If you fish responsibly, bass fishing can be a rewarding, lifelong hobby.

GLOSSARY

angler A person who fishes.

brackish Partly fresh, partly salt water.

contaminant A substance that adds impurities.

current Water moving continuously in a particular direction.

fiberglass A material made of glass particles fused together.

graphite A material made up of carbon fibers.

hatchling A small fish or animal recently hatched from an egg.

humane Showing sympathy or concern for others.

irrigate To supply with water by artificial means.

lactic acid An organic material that is created when carbohydrates are broken down in the body.

mimic To copy or imitate.

monofilament A single strand.

mucus A slick substance produced by the body to moisten and protect.

navigational device An instrument that aids in figuring out position, course, and distance traveled.

nylon A strong artificial substance.

organism A living person, plant, or animal.

predator An animal that kills other fish or animals.

reel A device set on the handle of a fishing pole to wind up or let out the fishing line.

replica A close or exact copy.

souvenir Something that serves as a reminder.

taxidermist Someone who prepares and mounts the skins of animals or fish.

Association of Fish and Wildlife Agencies
444 North Capitol Street NW, Suite 725
Washington, DC 20001
(202) 624-7890
Web site: http://www.fishwildlife.org
The Association of Fish and Wildlife Agencies represents North
America's fish and wildlife agencies and promotes management
and conservation of fish and wildlife.

Bass Federation Junior Anglers
2300 East Coleman Road
Ponca City, OK 74604
(580) 765.9031
Web site: http://bassfederation.com/tbf-youth/tbf-junior-anglers
The Junior Anglers program of the Bass Federation allows anglers
aged eleven to eighteen to be part of local bass fishing clubs.

Canadian Sportfishing Industry Association (CSIA)
1434 Chemong Road, Unit 11
Peterborough, ON K9J 6X2
Canada
(705) 745-8433
Web site: http://www.csia.ca
The CSIA works to preserve fishing opportunities for Canada's residents
and visitors. This is accomplished through education and management.

Collegiate Bass Anglers Association (CBAA)
4432 Olive Road
Plymouth, IN 46563

Web site: http://www.collegiatebass.org
CBAA's goal is to get young people interested in angling to keep the
sport of fishing alive for future generations.

FishAmerica Foundation
225 Reinekers Lane, Suite 420
Alexandria, VA 22314
(703) 519-9691
Web site: http://fishamerica.org
FishAmerica is working to preserve sportfish populations and keep
waters healthy in the United States and Canada.

Fisheries and Oceans Canada
200 Kent Street
13th Floor, Station 13E228
Ottawa, ON K1A 0E6
Canada
(613) 993-0999
Web site: http://www.dfo-mpo.gc.ca/index-eng.htm
This is Canada's official site for information on all fish-related topics
in Canada.

Lady Bass Anglers Association (LBAA)
774 Sugar Creek Road
Grand River, KY 42045
(540) 239-7902
Web site: http://www.ladybassanglers.com
LBAA's goal is to create professional fishing programs for women, and
to get more young women interested in the sport.

National Bass Anglers Association (NBAA Bass)
2532 Barber Road
Hastings, MI 49058
(269) 838-9482
Web site: http://www.nbaa-bass.com
NBAA Bass sponsors bass fishing tournaments and provides resources
for finding local bass fishing clubs.

National Oceanic and Atmospheric Administration (NOAA)
Fisheries Service
1315 East West Highway
Silver Spring, MD 20910
Web site: http://www.nmfs.noaa.gov
The NOAA Fisheries Service is in charge of protecting the marine
resources of the United States.

Professional Anglers Association (PAA)
P.O. Box 655
1102 Main Street
Benton, KY 42025
(270) 527-2030
Web site: http://fishpaa.com
The PAA aims to provide education to anglers to increase interest in
the sport and promote good conservation practices.

Recreational Boating and Fishing Foundation (RBFF)
500 Montgomery Street, Suite 300
Alexandria, VA 22314
(703) 519-0013

Web site: http://www.takemefishing.org
RBFF's mission is to increase the number of people who responsibly
    fish and boat.

U.S. Environmental Protection Agency (EPA)
Ariel Rios Building
1200 Pennsylvania Avenue NW
Washington, DC 20460
(202) 272-0167
Web site: http://www.epa.gov
The EPA is in charge of protecting humans and our natural
    environment—air, water, and land.

Web Sites

Due to the changing nature of Internet links, Rosen Publishing has
developed an online list of Web sites related to the subject of this
book. This site is updated regularly. Please use this link to access
the list:

http://www.rosenlinks.com/fish/bass

Beatty, Richard. *Rivers, Lakes, Streams, and Ponds*. Mankato, MN: Heinemann-Raintree, 2010.

Calhoun, Yael, ed. *Conservation*. New York, NY: Chelsea House Publications, 2005.

Fehl, Pamela. *Green Careers: Environment and Natural Resources*. New York, NY: Ferguson Publishing, 2010.

Fridell, Ron. *Protecting the Earth's Water Supply*. Minneapolis, MN: Lerner Publications, 2008.

George, Jean Craighead. *Pocket Guide to the Outdoors*. New York, NY: Dutton Children's Books, 2009.

Greenland, Paul R., and AnnaMarie L. Sheldon. *Career Opportunities in Conservation and the Environment*. New York, NY: Checkmark Books, 2008.

Hauge, Steve. *The Big Book of Bass: Strategies for Catching Largemouth and Smallmouth*. Minneapolis, MN: Creative Publishing International, 2008.

Hopkins, Ellen. *Fly Fishing*. Mankato, MN: Capstone Press, 2008.

Jones, Kevin. *Knowing Bass: The Scientific Approach to Catching More Fish*. Guilford, CT: The Lyons Press, 2005.

Kaye, Cathryn Berger, and Philippe Cousteau. *Going Blue: A Teen Guide to Saving Our Oceans, Lakes, Rivers, and Wetlands*. Minneapolis, MN: Free Spirit Publishing, 2010.

Labignan, Italo. *Hook, Line, and Sinker: Everything Kids Want to Know About Fishing*. Toronto, ON, Canada: Key Porter Books, 2007.

Martin, Roland. *Roland Martin's 101 Bass-Catching Secrets*. New York, NY: Skyhorse Publishing, 2008.

Newkirk, Ingrid. *The PETA Practical Guide to Animal Rights*. New York, NY: St. Martin's Griffin, 2009.

Popular Mechanics. *How to Tempt a Fish: A Complete Guide to Fishing*. New York, NY: Hearst Books, 2008.

Salas, Laura Purdie. *Saltwater Fishing*. Mankato, MN: Capstone Press, 2008.

Savik, Karen. *Bass: Use the Secrets of the Pros to Catch More and Bigger Bass*. Guilford, CT: The Lyons Press, 2008.

Schofeld, Jo, and Fiona Danks. *Go Wild! 101 Things to Do Outdoors Before You Grow Up*. London, England: Frances Lincoln, 2009.

Slade, Suzanne. *Let's Go Fishing*. New York, NY: Powerkids Press, 2007.

Underwood, Lamar, ed. *1001 Fishing Tips: The Ultimate Guide to Finding and Catching More and Bigger Fish*. New York, NY: Skyhorse Publishing, 2010.

Walker, Andrew. *How to Improve at Fishing*. New York, NY: Crabtree Publishing, 2009.

Burnley, Eric. *The Ultimate Guide to Striped Bass Fishing: Where to Find Them, How to Catch Them*. Guilford, CT: The Lyons Press, 2006.

Clouser, Bob. *Fly-Fishing for Smallmouth*. Mechanicsburg, PA: Stackpole Books, 2007.

George, Jean Craighead. *Pocket Guide to the Outdoors*. New York, NY: Dutton Children's Books, 2009.

Greenland, Paul R., and AnnaMarie L. Sheldon. *Career Opportunities in Conservation and the Environment*. New York, NY: Checkmark Books, 2008.

Labignan, Italo. *Hook, Line, and Sinker: Everything Kids Want to Know About Fishing*. Toronto, ON, Canada: Key Porter Books, 2007.

Newkirk, Ingrid. *The PETA Practical Guide to Animal Rights*. New York, NY: St. Martin's Griffin, 2009.

Popular Mechanics. *How to Tempt a Fish: A Complete Guide to Fishing*. New York, NY: Hearst Books, 2008.

Rose, David. *The Fishing Boat: Use the Secrets of the Pros to Select and Outfit Your Boat*. Guilford, CT: The Lyons Press, 2009.

Schultz, Ken. *Ken Schultz's Essentials of Fishing*. Hoboken, NJ: John Wiley & Sons, 2010.

Underwood, Lamar, ed. *1001 Fishing Tips: The Ultimate Guide to Finding and Catching More and Bigger Fish*. New York, NY: Skyhorse Publishing, 2010.

U.S. Environmental Protection Agency. *Guidance for Implementing the January 2001 Methylmercury Water Quality Criterion*. Washington, DC: U.S. Environmental Protection Agency, 2010.

INDEX

About the Author

Simone Payment has a degree in psychology from Cornell University and a master's degree in elementary education from Wheelock College. She is the author of twenty-five books for young adults. Her book *Inside Special Operations: Navy SEALs* (also from Rosen Publishing) won a 2004 Quick Picks for Reluctant Young Readers award from the American Library Association and is on the Nonfiction Honor List of Voice of Youth Advocates.

About the Consultant

Contributor Benjamin Cowan has more than twenty years of both fresh and saltwater angling experience. In addition to being an avid outdoorsman, Cowan is also a member of many conservation organizations. He currently resides in west Tennessee.

Photo Credits

Cover, pp. 1, 3 J&L Images/Photodisc/Getty Images; p. 7 © www.istockphoto.com/ Nicholas Belton; pp. 10, 24, 26 Shutterstock; p. 11 © St. Petersburg Times/Zuma Press; p. 13 © www.istockphoto.com/Richard Gunion; p. 16 iStockphoto/Thinkstock; p. 18 Wally Eberhart/Botanica/Getty Images; p. 21 Ron Brooks; p. 22 Ronald C. Mondra/ Sports Imagery/Getty Images Sport/Getty Images; pp. 29, 37, 39 Ronnie Garrison; p. 31 Sam Diephuis/Stone/Getty Images; p. 34 © www.istockphoto.com/Lawrence Sawyer; p. 41 Wisconsin Department of Natural Resources; p. 44 Rusty Hill/FoodPix/ Getty Images; p. 46 © www.istockphoto.com/John Tomaselli; p. 49 Lisa Dejong/ The Plain Dealer/Landov; p. 52 © David R. Frazier/The Image Works; back cover and interior graphics (silhouette) © www.istockphoto.com/A-Digit; (green grass) © www. istockphoto.com/Makhnach M; (waves) © www.istockphoto.com/Michael Jay.

Designer: Nicole Russo; Editor: Nicholas Croce;
Photo Researcher: Marty Levick